T0328532

JUST THINKING

Collection of Poems

———◆———

VOLUME 2

JUST THINKING
Collection of Poems

———✦———

Volume 2

Abimbola Mosobalaje Davis

Safari Books Ltd
Ibadan

Published by

Safari Books Ltd
Ile Ori Detu
1, Shell Close
Onireke, Ibadan.
Email: safarinigeria@gmail.com
Website: www.safaribooksng.com

In association with:

Books & Sports Limited
15, Mahogany Way,
Forest Hill Estate,
Jericho GRA,
Ibadan, Oyo State.
Website: www.booksandsportsng.com
Email: info@booksandsportsng.com
Tel: +23422913964

© 2015, Abimbola Mosobalaje Davis

First Published 2015

ISBN: 978-978-8431-90-9

DEDICATION

To Mama, Apinke, and all women of this world,
the goddesses without shrines.

Contents

FOREWORD

A bimbola Mosobalaje Davis, the author of *Just Thinking, Vol I*, has followed up the brilliant collection with *Just Thinking, Vol II*, demonstrating renewed passion, skill and a more versatile approach to the presentation of societal decadence in diverse forms in Nigeria specifically and the world at large.

The dominating theme of this volume is the political predicament in the Nigerian system, though applicable to other systems in the world. As demonstrated in Volume I, the poet's commitment to political stability in Nigeria is projected in 'Tenses lost in senses,' which is about the politically generated insecurity in Nigeria; 'Future,' an admonition to treasury looting politicians; 'Untouchable,' which addresses the political godfather syndrome and 'Vanity,' which is a reflection on the vain glory of the corrupt and power-hungry politicians. Other poems with political themes are 'Mayhem in the city,' which addresses the political cataclysms caused by few powerful politicians while 'Lies and Truth' focus on politicians' mendacity. In addition, In you Arthur,' 'Predicaments,' 'Now that He is Frail' and 'Scent of a Woman' all present the incessant confusion, sadness and pains caused by those in government and the illegitimate wealth they amass. To Davis, our "Leadership (is) in trouble undulation" and the "generation unborn (is) in subjugation." However, he does not only state the problems but, as prophetic as a poet could be, forecasts a looming revolution, calling out the spirits of his heroes to "reject these leaders of woes!"

Just Thinking Volume II also features terrorism and its blurred distorted principles. 'In Wrong War' and 'Principles in Jigsaw,' Davis emphasises the confusions about Boko Haram terrorists' ideas and philosophy. Other themes include motivation and mentorship. 'The Mindset,' a poem that encourages the youths to face life and its roughness and *'Privilege,'* which extols the virtues of great teachers whom one could easily identify as mentors to Davis in his creative voyage, are both motivational. Like the Yoruba traditional poet, he sings the praises of great creative writers such as Tanimu Abubakar, Femi Osofisan, John Pepper Clark-Bekederemo, Cyprian Ekwensi, Wole Soyinka and Niyi Osundare as a mark of respect and a bow to prosper. In the same vein, Davis acknowledges the Headmaster's' tutelage and his hard work in 'Headmaster.'

Mosobolaje Davis revisits the pleasure of loving in the poems 'Weak Heart' and 'Love Rhythms,' and the pains of a failed marriage in 'Divorce.' Other societal vices such as fraud, cultism, unemployment and hunger also inspired him in 'Oluwole,' 'Admission,' 'No easy Day' and 'Hunger.'

Mosobolaje Davis' knowledge of Yoruba history comes to play in his poetic verses. 'In Moremi,' he retells a Yoruba legendary tale, connecting it to the present and calling for peace at Ile-Ife so that the pains of the goddess who sacrificed her only child for societal peace will not be in vain.

Overall, *'Just Thinking Volume II'* is another well composed collection of poems that should be owned by all. It is moralistic, informative and didactic. I strongly recommend the collection for personal use and academic purposes.

Adenike Akinjobi (PhD)
Associate Professor of English
University of Ibadan
Nigeria

PREFACE

When the first warhead was fired, the salvo, urege to trudge on was mustered, perhaps by the euphoria of acceptance of my first work, stoked both by friends and foes alike, thus, the decision to write this second volume *'Just Thinking –Collection of Poems, Volume II'*, the title created out of boredom in opulence and advantages drived out of ineptitude. Or maybe, stories adopted before sailing into dementia or Nigerian syndrome, forgetfulness of the facts of the pasts. Simles

Come to think of it, it amuses when I realised they now call me an author, a blab and blabbing made rich by the indolence of frail minds that refused to read from their pasts but now paid for stories retold by a greenhorn! What do I know that you don't? Really nothing, except that we all retell old folklores in new ways and become noble, an act or attitude of craze celebrated amongst humorous compatriots. When stealing from our common heritage became a norm, results of your forgetfulness and ignorance, or stubbornness and refusal to take to *ijala, esa* and *rara* of the Yoruba, the *udu, ekwe* drums and *oja* flute of the Igbos or *kalangu, goje* and *waka* of the Hausas, blowing them at their criminal minds and faces!

The more reasons we will pay more, especially the academics, for their continuum satirical liturgy, because we stoked our broods to learn, listen and celebrate rather than mourn the dearth of our morals, culture and heritage! Or maybe we are too puffy, arrogant and abstract to apologise and start with our wards and home fronts, thus making useless my thinking, or at least, helping me from sinking in thinking. Thoughts, if you like!

This collection is a continuation of my soul still thinking, searching and still collecting, like a madman and his foray on the field, searching and collecting barbs. Before committing perfidy in outrage and protest against the society, lest I'm accused of the similitude of acts I loathe, I chose to venture into the second volume, celebrating the first and yielding to the requests, from my solitude.

Just Thinking – Collection of Poems: Volume II is a trial after my independence, a confluence of poems written with confidence. I hope you will enjoy and share in my agonies and sometimes, happiness.

Abimbola Mosobalaje Davis
Ibadan.
2015.

ACKNOWLEDGEMENTS

My gratitude goes to Adenike Akinjobi, Associate Professor of English Phonology, Department of English, University of Ibadan, for her tireless efforts and invaluable contributions to this book. Her disarming smiles and encouragement go beyond the face but to the mind. Her 'tutorial' on words and punctuations, those little signs that would have turned the poems to prose and meanings to jargons, the reminder of my school days, is appreciated. Professor Akinjobi demonstrated her prowess, as a teacher who chose to set the beads, lace it and only asked me to beat the drum. Thank you, Prof, *Omo owa 'moekun laofin li'Ogo Ekiti* (The offspring of Owa, the daughter of the Lion in the Palace at Igogo-Ekiti).

As usual, my wife, Olayinka, has always been there for me. Her cooperation can be very troubling, wondering if she would burst and cry of neglect, but she never did. Rather, she encouraged me to forge ahead, most often coming up with ideas to work on. Jokingly, she would say, *'mofe d'aya akowe'*, "I want to become a wife of an author." Thank you, Darling; here is the 'Akowe' of your dreams and the result of your sleepless nights.

The trilogy,' The Book', is about the first book 'Just Thinking – Collection of Poems', and an introduction to this Volume.

The Book

I.

When I wrote those stanzas
And I moulded those tenses
And he gave those blessings
For my few senses,

I knew those verses
Would bring more chances
Or, and little clashes
But my little gambles

And the dirty rabbles
With my little hustle
No need to have a tousle
Or goggle to read my bundle

II.

Try, less I am fried
But shame not in trying
To whom efforts yield
Heaven gives some grace

Prayer, truly is good
Difficult it is to pray
But to whom success smiles
Heaven makes its friend

But happy is a man
Whom heaven makes a friend
For all things he knows
When heaven made happen

III.

Let me die in attempt
For I am in success trying
Like ants attempt a hill
To build and touch the tilt

Build your castle not in the air
So say the sages of the ages
But this age has since denied
Architects built in the air.

When I wrote those stanzas
And I moulded those tenses
And he gave those blessings
Heaven made me its kindred.

O, bearer of new tower
Be careful of town criers
The fall of last Commanders
Before the arrival of pall bearers

(Culled from 'Colours In My Rhythms')

This poem was inspired by late Dr. Tai Solarin's article, 'May Your Road Be Rough.'
The Mindset was written to inspire the youths to prepare them for the future.

The Mindset

As the sunset
You and your mindset
Right from the onset
In the midst of the best set
Shall be rough till the next set
So said the sage first, but
Aftermath of our mindsets
When legs set forth to the set crest
And our friends with no blotch
In our midst was no splotch
That our mind has brought forth
But why would our race be so wrought
And our worth so daubed?
From the onset of our mindset
But the words of the old sage
That our road will be so rough!

About the potty bank of my youth

My Bank

My life and my savings
You fanciful clay pot
Black or brown or this nature
Dark corner, the grace in aloofness

The ornament from the herbal store
Antiquities, herbal seller and huge leaves
Goat heads, animal legs and cowries
The fear of the herbal woman

Afore the pot, my lot and coins
Were all for rusk
'Not like the thrift'- Mama Oyo
Never spend all your savings

This purse, this pot and my cup
The enthuse for the kidding crush
Gifts and rakes of my early rush
The pot of my foundation

But now grown I am
Post and prowl, the Banks growl
Accumulation for my savings
Remembrance of my brown pot

Dedication to all women on Mother's Day

The Woman

You are a goddess without a shrine
The mystery we all adore.

The woman,
That myth in your look
Which men gaze at in awe
To see your face and gape in waves
In whom, resides the world we live.

The woman,
The wisdom embroidered by your age
Sad not or whistle for wrinkles in your face
Because in that wrinkles are my kindles.

The woman,
With whom strangeness lives and bore
But whom the envy of men abhor
But you, she treats with love.

The woman,
Beginning of life with death adores
The conqueror of men and his bluffs
The fertility he envies.

The woman,
To whom affection snoozes and oozes
Yet in passion, the man made whore
To whom forgiveness made a goddess.
The scent of love you are
Woman, a goddess without a shrine.

When Justice is spineless
Judge muses in silence
Like a gong filled in mustard
Cry not, the beat is on

(Culled from 'Colours In My Rhythms'

Against insecurity in the country caused by strange indoctrinations and deadly political upheavals

Tenses Lost In Sense

Life and its histories
Reasons for its mysteries
But searching for its essence
Tenses lost in senses

Brawls and the brothers
Sadness for their mothers
But peace eludes their members
Tenses lost in senses

Encroachment of our colonies
Quandaries and banditries
Like a country lost her boundaries
Tenses lost in senses

Written to extol the virtues of great teachers like Tanimu Abubakar, Femi Osofisan, John Pepper Clark-Bekederemo, Cyprian Ekwensi, Wole Soyinka and Niyi Osundare

14

The Privilege

I

In whom would I unyoke this desire?
The dwelling spirit of a writer
The mind that roves and flutters
Whose wandering needs a vessel
Tanimu, Osofisan, or Bekederemo
In whose league I craved like a suitor
But age and right to be tutored
They claimed the age is the mirror
Whose language the joy of the words
But this language I sought in haste
Before my gloat to waste
To groove, to mold, to dwell.

II

Fail not to say, true are my words
That in you, my heart pours its pure
That the sorrow I lived, your tomorrow to reap
Forget not the deep, my experience to guide
In them lays your beginning, but my end
For joy of your generation, the privilege made for you
For your tomorrow to bliss, my yesterday I gave
Laugh not my child, your tomorrow he awaits
Forget not the rights to give, privilege you took

In the pool of these ponds, the pains of my mind
From the blackness of my pot, beget you white pap
Your tomorrow he awaits: your right to give.

III

But this privilege that I own
And the right to be known
When mind yields to the throne
Not the style that I'm versed
Nor the carriage I was stacked
Or the tutelage once bemoaned
Cyprian, Soyinka or Osundare
These purveyors of the words
Their guides and my losses
To bloom, to know and to mould
Like the kittens and their mother
In whose privilege the grace I culled

The crime of Eden, my mindset
Beauty of Eve, doubt in my mood
Naked is me with this robe
The gloat I crave, you to have
Blame me not, I'm Adam sucked

(Culled from 'Colours In My Rhythms')

'Future' is a warning to the politicians whose sole aim is to loot the treasury.

Future

The future he knew not
What awaits the victory?
The embellishment of his success
Position at the ballots
When he led his peer-harlots
But the desecration of the altar
That we thought was aura
Like the beauty of the flora
The shackles on the former
The Agency and his predecessor
Like the future and its secrets
Careful, or the man will falter

A godfather, his greed, his wealth and his pains

Untouchable

This world he holds
Like the power he boasts
All laws he broke
But who will cage this folk?

Not the capital he made
Nor the muscle of his mate
But his power is their gate
His villa, their haven,

Like a vessel and its anchorage
But the arrival of the heaven
Who knew not his sibling
Yesterday he conquered.

Today he moans,
Blessing is your sorrow;
That today will bless,
To the boastful and the cruel!

A short theological liturgy on the Holy Trinity, the Father, the Son and the Holy
Spirit, retold in a different version

The Trinity

The trust is you
Custodian of hope
Future He assured
Of you He made.

His hope in love
Friendship he doffed
Who else but you
The trinity?

And you the trinity
Like Him, he said
You, he made,
Then you: the trust.

The Father and His Spirit
But, in Him, you came
You and Him,
He, your father.

And living in you
The Spirit,
Then you, of Him,
The Trust.

'Harmattan' is about the harmattan season and the mood.

Harmattan

Little humid with constant whistles
Flurry, subtle, your harshly winds
Winds or myths with mystical bliss
Grayish days with mind waves
Glum the rhythms lost in haste
When tanning becomes a caste
And bathing loathed like leech
Men in harem with crackled flame
Blistered lips and leached nose
Nature and man in thrilling tango
Harmattan is but, a gut-cracker
When men glint like Halloween.

This poem is about Nigeria, the politicians and their looting cronies, the sadness and pains and the looming revolution!

Scent of a Woman

There lives a woman
In a village of the West
Besides where lake amazes
Where torrents do crashes
Her tender hand waves the maize
To buy or eat and free your hunger
By her side lays her kits
The woods, the coals, the matches
In her eyes lives the kindness
Happy, her hut waits on her baby
The one the maize will make a maid
But the passersby, is a man of leisure
He trots, bluffs, and clutches her maize
In happiness, she gave her grace
But the man is but a load of blades
Her lace, he grooved and bolted like mice
To the runner of her treasure
Sad, the woman besides the lake
She'll grunt, smiles and squirms!
Until her curse arrests the swine.

Reminiscences about my growing up at the Headmaster's house in Ibadan

Headmaster

Life of a teacher
Teacher in my matter
Before my alma mater
Learning of the stanza

Trouble or you are humble
Our house in rumble
House built by his bundle
Clever or be humbled!

Head of my masters
Master, we thundered
When is your siesta?
Our season headmaster
In you I was mastered.

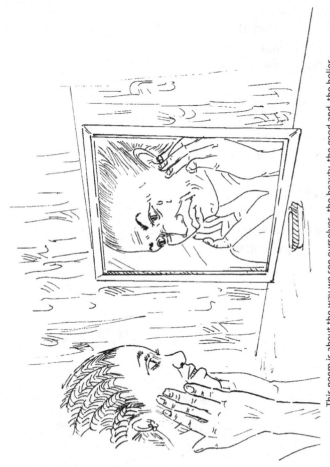

This poem is about the way we see ourselves, the beauty, the good and, the holier than thou attitudes in us: the opposite of which we are!

Mirror

My hair and the wetness
Drizzling of water, this chest
The kissing waves, my neck
The smoothness, not my face
But these pimples and the dimples
The scales and my teeth
And the contours on my temple
Lone catwalks in my washroom
'Hello' from my eyebrows
'How are you?' that my lips sing
A little display of madness
Alone but not homeless
Mirror without the frizzles
Lies and mind in grizzles
Secrets within my muscles
Those evils that are bristled
That love, my heart rekindled
Perhaps, coyness of my sly
Mirrors don't tell the truth
Methinks, secret is the mirror.

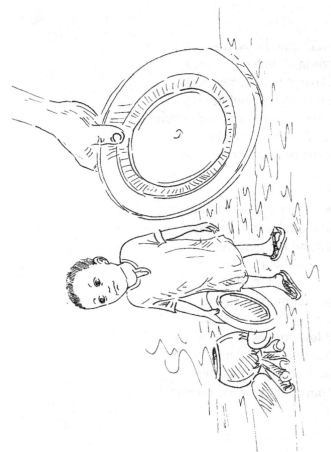

This poem is about the austere time and the attitude of people.

Hunger

When the kettle whistles
And the water drizzles
Cook or lose the vapour
Before vapour fans to moisture
While stomach cries and cringes
And motion refuses fling
The timidity on the ring
And the heart in contention
Not the Lectern for Messiah
But the stomach and desire
Why mouth drools and tire
As soul beckons to nature
Siege unto visitor
The urge in the stomach
Not because he's a miser
Nothing, but the hunger.

Sleep and the dreams

Sleep

Few hours of my death
When you took me off the sphere
When I became a flying dove
Seven seas I crossed
Several miles I traversed
Briefly made an errand king
Supplications to the higher King
In harmony, the choir sings
In ring death did sing
Except those with little snags
But he said we all play death
When sleep gives a little rest.

This is about the principle of Boko Haram's terrorism.

Principle in *Jigsaw*

In whom lies the spirit of hate
To rake and rave, and bait
To whom is the power reposed
To halt in adolescent, the girls!

The alteration of generation next
And neighbours in disorderliness
Wars for their stubbornness
And hatred for their loathness.

Ideologies or dreams lost
When baits are sibling of yours
And demystification of your gods
When blood and temple you trod!

The alterations in the altars
And the stains of the sacredness!
The words you commune, you loath
Tarry, of what principles you war!

*Aladuras - Orthodox Christians.
This a metaphorically, expresses the political uncertainties in Nigeria.

Predicaments

The gentleness of the sea
Dancing rhythms of its waves
Celebration of its royalty
Where spirits display their artistry
Singing mangrove of its harbours
When dolphins disrupts its colours
Raging booms of the Aladuras
But, the innocence of the crabs
Whose fates end before sunset
Wales, sharks, rage for little pests
Or the arrival of the tempest
When spatter of water informs
Farmers and fishermen beware
Beneath the water, soil rises
Whose noon bleed in crises
Hopes died in flurry of vanity!

A Lovers' poem

Weak Heart

Methinks, my world at war
That of love and war
War, not of blood
But of war in passion

And of love to motion
I thought I was a stallion
That fears not to war
But of love to brood

In prayer to be my hood
But here I am your stooge
The tickling for my weakling
The power of your loving.

About a political kingpin with terminal ailment and his illegal wealth

Now That He Is Frail

His heart now frail
And his hands now weak
Now that he knows
The vanity of his heist
And the penalty of his sins
Now that he knows
That death is his gain
Troubles of his past
The bedrock of his sins
The betrayal of his kin
To be a man he harms
With lots of tricks he charm
Our treasure he claimed
But his heart is frail
And his hands are weak
Behold, his greed but my loss!

The trilogy mused about vanity and questions for the desperate, the corrupt and power-hungry politicians.

Vanity

I.

Despite my wrappers
And the tightness of my girdle
I can still feel my nakedness
Reasons for my helplessness

Despite my struggles
And survival of the troubles
I can still see the huddle
Reasons for being humble

Despite my freedom
And the gallantry of my fiefdom
I can still feel the captivity
Reason why it's all vanity

II.

Celebration of his success
That one they hail, conquest
Stocks for future bequest
Before quest turns to inquest

Celebration in his action
Like a prisoner and his ration
When action gone auction

Nods in constant motion
Despite my freedom
And the gallantry of my fiefdom
I can still feel the captivity
Reason why it's all vanity

III.

When wealth toils health
And health stuck opulence
Reason for labour befuddles
When death baits man

When death dances in puzzle
And honour lost in muddle
Reason why rich reeks to fear
Like a man caught in war

But this wealth and health
Opulence and honour befuddled
When death caught its game
Labour and man in vanity

When lies, in foundation he told
Vengeance brought now in folds
Grief, trouble and regret
O, kindred I know they are

(Culled from 'Colours In My Rhythms')

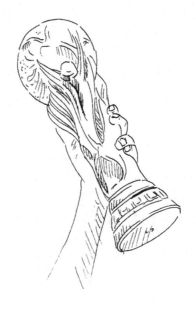

Written to celebrate the national football team, the Green Eagles, when they won the African Nations Cup

The Race

Do not cry, losing in the race
Your beginning in the race
Is your winning of the race

When you lost the ace
You have given to the mace
Or faze and you fail
When your race is to be gauged

Your making of the race
Is the secret of the game
And the rule of the race
Not the losing at the game
But the belief in the game

Stop not from the race
Or refuse to participate
But race on with the pace
Because a winner of the race
Pace to know about the race
They live to race for the gain.

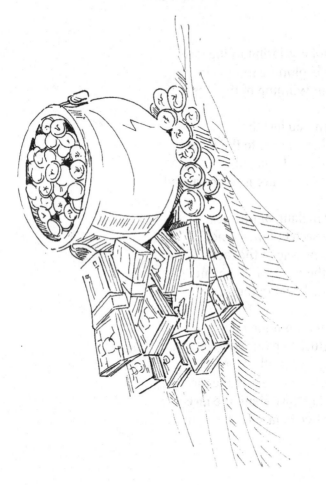

This poem was inspired by Khalil Gibran's book, "The Prophet." It is about the philosophy of life.

Fortune

Sad not when you lose some fortunes
For loss and gain are kindred
A driver to the other

In your sadness lives your happiness
The one to which you are born
From her pain you were brought
In blood and water, happiness of her mating

Pray not for misfortune
Happy not in your fortune
For pains lives in fortune
The fortune that misfortune begot

But remember the misfortune
That brought you the fortune
For unguarded fortune, brings you misfortune
A driver to the other.

Inspired by Khalil Gibran's perception of the relationship between death and man

The Death

At the masked one, they raged!
The one with the power to take
The masked one with cold hands!
The trusted and the beloved of his Master

But upset you not, at the masked one
The messenger and his messages
For in him lives the essence of life
Sibling of same parents, Life and Death

One to give, one to take, but one to hate
They are the twins, we, third of them
The masked one, the life and us
Triplet we are, Life, you and the masked one.

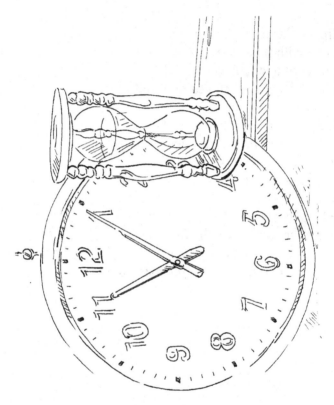

This poem is about the reading of time by man: the conflicts and the resolutions.

Time

Of the seasons and our delusion
When man birthed the time
The galas between man and fallacy
Intention to tame by invention

But one thing we knew, our decisions
AST, EST, GMT, CAT, our contraptions
Conception of time, an aberration
In those decisions we are in suspicion

In you live the time, your illusion
The strand of your hair, not your decision
Weakness of your feet, like transition

In that delicateness of your soles
And the wariness of our souls
The fragility of my fingers
Disability of intentions, in inventions
The fade of these delusions.

Political upheaval caused by the ambitions of a few

Mayhem in the City

Awake the spirits of my heroes
The city you built is mourning
Streets and songs of mayhem
Oh Guardians of my tomorrow!
But today we are in sorrow
Discoveries of men in furore
Votes they sought with horror
Maim and rage, their odour
Like fire in dried thatched roof
Madness in action or mutilation
Leadership in trouble undulation
Generation unborn in subjugation
Aberration to class litigation
Honour in mourning reiteration
Awake the spirits of my heroes
To reject these leaders of woes!

The goddess, Moremi, and the sacrifice of her only daughter, Oluorogbo, for peace, but the peace that has eluded Ife because of politics

Moremi

O great woman of valour
Your mettle and your spirit
For the love of the city
We doubt not your beauty

The burden and the crown
Your bravery and the conquest
But the city and her quest
Your courage and the death

Descendants and the strangers
The sacrifice of Oluorogbo
The deaD and the royal
But betrayal by the loyal

In vain now is your valour
Your city, descendants of rages
Like a broiler, bred to waste
Sadness for the goddess!

A lovers' poem

Love Rhythms

1. Groom

Not yet to go?
Where else to sow?
Who else to hold?
Your mind, for mine

It's you and yours
That I owe my love
To hold and own
My love, you are

Behold, I know
You kiss, to kill
The pains, your heart
The shield, I crave

Desire to hold,
The warmth and folds
Where else to go
To you, I propose

II. Bride's Cry

Today I'm happy yet I'm sad
New name in array of rites
Twist the face of faith

Of twain to race to fate
Whole she-goat, fruits in row
Honey, umbrella and Bible in tow
When family dances in culture suck
Family lost in wedlock crush
Standing chairman and the cheerleader
One family in dowry fish to share
Sad I am in investment flare
Like a permafrost in thaw
Cry I am of the father lost
The fees, the school; the feeds he lost
But a ring they brought, his daily toils
Whereupon the family in jaw-jaw joy
Dowry was taken to bond the change
His name, his rights, away they took
In compliance of change his name I took
But truly what befalls his name
That a stranger will make to change
The culture of bond is why I'm sad

III. The Rite

Shoosh! Now in mating mood
Not working to energy sap
But the culture of hold and wrap
Emotion of love in joyful flap
Like fact of life and treasure hunt
Not of gold: or diamond lust
But of lust the parents gulped
When in joy of woman's wit
Once a secret before it's known

The rite of passage done and blown
Not me: but the oath our Adam blew
But toil, mate, suffer and reel in lust
Crush, lust, cause, axioms of Eve
When in Eden he burst to grief
To breed descendant of ancient myth
Shoosh! Now in mating mood

The peacock and the mating process

Jariel, my Peacock

My blue bird with its fine crown
Satin blue and your beaded face
The dancing pearls of your neck
Jariel, those silky covert feathers
When you run from the fletcher
But your fear and the trust
When I named you Jariel
Flannel of your armpits
Adornment and your beaded neck
Piercing calls to the peahen
When you are in fan flaunt to flirt
Life of my Jariel.

Politicians and lies about their educational qualifications

Lies

I know I'm not read
But bet, I have bread
Lie not to get head
The lies will come rest
The lie you brought forth
Will turn and mud you
He knew he had none
Why lies of those horns
Your pride and those lies
Disgrace in quick pace
When lies do come forth
You are a non-sought.

Education, cultism and success

Admission

I.

I was uncertain
That I was here
They did make some fun
Of my little known fate
When I saw that result
I was still unsure
It was my admission
Road to this citadel, but
Siblings made some fun
And less admired
But truly I'm here
To learn and admire

II.

The hell or friends I will make
To stay the fury of their rage
Nocturnal group and their loop
Rejection of their calls, you good, or
Crying will be me, and my mission
When admission turned omission
Like the rage and fury of the axe
Before the oath and their hoax
This fraternity youth do kiss

To joy, but future to go astray
But truly here I am
To learn, admire, and pass

III.

Of hero known I am
That citadel brought and nurtured
Not hero hoped and lost
The outcome of peer denied
The admission to my mission
The mission of my vision
When you denied their oath
The hero in you is spurred
To rule and mould the world
Like rainbow blinks the sky
But truly here I am
The hero known I'm here

When life stutters and fumbles
And dreams seemed to tumble
When mouth grazes to stutter
Then the race to life is mustered
Run not, race awaits your order

(Culled from 'Colours In My Rhythms')

When business goes awful

The Road

This road I've passed
This road I knew
Sagged, my memory wanes
Albeit, memory never lies
Oh, the road I've known
But when mind troves
Extra terrestrial or spiritual
The one I travelled unknown
The road so hollow
Mind stay wallow
Why spirit in welter
Of the road I've passed.

About the complexity of the night

Night

Darkness is a grace
To love or to fear
The trails of the spirits
The musing of the fallen
Darkness of the night
Fear as its grace!

Like the queen of the night
Flowers and its fragrance
Freedom and the brazen
In the darkness of the night
Love conjure or misadventure
Scents of love.

Mysteries of their movements
Secrets of the monuments
Shrines and the slimes
The secret of the darkness
Be careful of the darkness
Fear as its grace!

The warm to behold
And the kiss untold
The secret of the rites
The travelling of the stars
Wandering of the moon
Scents of love.

Certificate scandal

The Truth

Don't ask me why
My pains and these sorrows
These mysteries and the sobs
When soul soiled in shrub
Slurs the life, the elder's lies
When in tender, the elder slimes
Slandered am I, the baby cries
Life in reek, gunge and goop
Fake are you, the lies under book
When stormy gone the certificate
Not surprised of the scandal
Just their latest blunder.

Confusion about Boko Haram's ideas and philosophy

Wrong Wars

In wrong wars or words of wrong men
Their words burn straws, like mote kills soul
We wail when innocent bent, when wronged men life lost
In war of wrong wars their words draw war
When flake the hake in the lake, hate is blood
Body bags and trough blocked, when war in market draw
Life of kids mute when the wrong got caught!
Of man, woman and child innocents, but life naught
Lives, termite sought in body bags when trough blocked
When stomach turned, mind dozed and fresh lily slopped
Of lost principles, when Delilah miffed
This musing, dirge for the living, is Samson's lost!
    But they are no crusaders; but herds with no charm,
    When they crammed, lost are they before their clan.

Divorce and the pains

Divorce

Once you knew, your love I craved
Before the rage, haze and rave
Our love proclaimed, here and there
Agreement to hell or den.

The melting of hearts, truth repelled
Sad, we noticed, but not the force
Forces ignored, butour faults
Our years before, now a waste!

The vacuum and the kids, the space
That suffering for kids, will rotate
Like the fallacy we told, of the late
For this I wished, but to wait

To take the pains, pale, but stay
But this divorce, is your crave
Like a hand, that is stained,
The covenant we vowed, is but fake.

The hate to love, your desire
Hold agony or love, or I retire
But the faith I lost, is my fate
The divorce I loathe, is my take!

Bishop Oluwole Street in Lagos where fraud and fake documents thrive

Oluwole

Of hero and road bestowed
But lo, clone was honed.

In the capital of our star
It means God has entered
But why men deterred?
We gaped in awe.

To whom courage enamoured
Garlands for the armour.

Counterfeit, hoax, in the street
Chomp, munch the tyros
Oh crunch! This group of warps
Where greed baits in synchrony.

Kingpins, rings and covert
O, boulevard and its simulators
Parodists, crimes by its aggregators
Name dishonoured by his broods!

Unemployed graduate and his predicament

No Easy Day

No easy day
Mirage! warned, my teacher
Fantasy of my ecstasy
Salivating on my libation
Celebration of my graduation
I sang, danced and drank
The future now in motion
But the visions now illusion
Like a farmer lost the season
The mind delusion to scorn
To work from dawn till worn
Nakedness of my day
But fantasy of my ecstasy
Truly, no easy day.

Man and his predicament; tracing it to the Garden of Eden where he betrayed God

Adam

Why is man so restless?
Win, loss, he rests not
Story of past, present; is Eden lost,
When He shares in His kindness?
But His name to blame!
The man he made to claim,
His Kingdom, but with norms!
Before immortal inverted
His greed or lust or perfidy
But now the race for His grace
To be the viceroy of the race
When race is gauged in rage
The age of white is beige
Betrayal by man and His covenant
The vow he broke to lust,
Of which the world must suffer!

In praise of Mother Africa

Africa

Lose not your identity
The one with which you are born
Mother of my ancestors
Why are your children flighty?
Your mother and mine

Mother of great mysteries
But why is your name in disdain
The reasons for our reap
Lost am I to leap
As they took my claim

But you cover my shame
When hope is lost in aims
My hope you fuelled
To hold, and know, and rope
My right to lope

Tenderly on your savannah
My right to grow
On this slushiness of your soil
From where mothers inherit
The fertility of their wombs

When stillbirth refused to twin
The waste, the life, the crumb
Africa, life and your rhythms
When nature fuels the aims
That makes you Africa.

Trembling my soul
In float my whole
Like a linen in the air
O, Sing to me, a lullaby

(Culled from 'Colours In My Rhythms')

Nigeria's political experience, history and caution to the country

In you, Arthur

I.

Oh, Arthur, friend of my reverie
Saw you sitting by the riverine
Dreamt of you and blueberry
The sublimity of its greenery
So close yet so far away
In you I had those future dreams
To walk the talk and hold the rock
But with you I have to run
Because with you, I'm just a dunce
Here I am, the rock you flung
Arthur, in you I had those dreams
But in you, I lost the dreams.

II.

When you asked for the reasons
The reason for my grizzles
When power refused to listen
And my life like your kitchen
The reason for the freezing
When I crouched like the kitten
My life baited, demeaning
Our meeting with no meaning
The meeting and the reasons
You said I was the reason
But the natives at the meeting

'Woe betide you, Arthur', they cried
Old people slumped in clamour
Promise to live or to die, Arthur
Albeit, promise of the blossom, I thought
But your deceits are the reasons!

III.

June 12th it was, when notion gave birth to contraptions
Arthur was the author, who nurtured the rupture
Amongst his cohorts, gravely the city was fractured
Davis the rotor, that turned the words to seizure
That world will claim to fan the rancour
Before Ibrahim and the seizure, fear of lead actor
Justice and the judges, who judged but not with justice
Nay! Deceits, sly or treachery, cacophony and the elders
Natives waited to tune, their aims not worn
Hold not the assembly, grave, this ides of May
The owner of the minds, twisted but whole mindset
Listen, or face the quagmire, blood of the crying solar
    Monarch and his contraptions, height of his infractions
    Be careful of the contingent, tractions in democracy

Printed in the United States
By Bookmasters